Published by Tughra Books

335 Clifton Ave., Clifton,
NJ, 07011, USA
www.tughrabooks.com

Noble Women of Faith

Written & Illustrated by
Shahada Sharelle Abdul Haqq

Text Edited by
Zeba Alam

ISBN 978-1-59784-268-6

NOBLE WOMEN OF FAITH
ASIYA, MARY, KHADIJA, FATIMA

SHAHADA SHARELLE ABDUL HAQQ

ASIYA: DAUGHTER OF MUZAHIM, WIFE OF THE PHARAOH

Asiya bint Muzahim, may God be pleased with her, grew up at a time of great oppression. Her father was Muzahim. The children of Israel's population was growing. One night, the Pharaoh, an evil Egyptian king, had an unusual dream. His fortune-tellers told him, "An Israelite boy will be born there, and he will destroy the kingdom of the Pharaoh."

The Pharaoh ordered every newborn Israelite baby to be killed, while he saved the girls. Asiya was among young girls of Israel who was spared, she happened to have been raised in a believing household.

When she grew up, the Pharaoh, one of the most evil men in history, heard of her beauty and wanted her as a slave. Her father begged him to marry her instead, because her treatment would be better as his wife. When Asiya's father told her she was to marry the Pharaoh, she was horrified. She asked, "How can I marry him?" Her father explained to her that if she did not marry him, he would kill their entire family. So she agreed to live as his wife even though she hated him and his oppression.

She lived as a believer, but kept her strong faith hidden. She had unlimited wealth at her disposal, and people worshipped her husband.

Asiya did not have children, and longed for a believing child. Around this time, Yukabid, the Hebrew mother of Moses, peace be upon him, gave birth to him, and through divine inspiration, she hid Moses in a chest, and put him into a river to save

him from being killed. The chest carrying the baby Moses ended up in front of the palace of the Pharaoh. Asiya asked her husband if they could keep the baby as a comfort to her eyes (Qasas 28:9). The Pharaoh said, "He may comfort your eyes, but not mine." Yet he agreed to let her keep him. As part of God's divine plan, the infant Moses would not accept milk from any wet nurse in the palace so he would cry. Finally the sister of Moses, who had been following the chest as it floated up the Nile River, said she knew of a lady whose milk he would accept. And so the mother of Moses, Yukabid, came to nurse him. He stopped crying, so both believing women raised Moses.

Prophet Moses received a nobleman's education in the palace. As he grew older, he came to realize the injustice the Egyptians inflicted upon the Israelites. One day he saw two men fighting, and in defending an Israeli man, he unintentionally killed an Egyptian.

Moses fled from Egypt in a state of fear and went to Midian walking in the dessert day and night with only the clothes on his back. He eventually married one of the daughters of Prophet Shuayb, peace be upon him. He did not have wealth, so he agreed to work in Shuayb's household in return for marrying his daughter.

After ten years when his term was completed, Moses decided to visit Asiya and his mother Yukabid, whom he missed very much. On his way, he received the revelation of the Torah from God on Mount Sinai. He first shared this news with his wife, then continued his journey to Egypt, and shared the revelation with Asiya and his mother. Both accepted the message immediately without question.

After a while, Asiya could not hide her faith from her husband, the Pharaoh. Part of believing in Moses meant she would have to migrate with the believers and children of Israel out of Egypt. The Pharaoh did not want anyone to leave, especially his wife. He told her she could not go with Moses, and tortured her in an attempt to make her give up her faith (*iman*). She did not give up.

Asiya's faith in God increased. She loved the Lord Most High with all her heart. When news of his wife's devotion to God reached the Pharaoh, he beat her and commanded his guards to beat her. They took her out in the scalding noon heat, tied her hands and feet, and beat her perpetually. She turned to none other than her Lord, God. She prayed, "My Lord! Build for me a home in Paradise in nearness to You, and keep and save me from the Pharaoh and his conduct; and save me from the wrongdoing people" (Tahrim 66:11). It was narrated that when she said this, the sky opened up for her and she saw her home in Paradise, and smiled.

The guards watched in astonishment: She's being tortured and she smiles? Frustrated, the Pharaoh commanded a boulder be brought and dropped on her to crush her to death. However, God, in His mercy, took her soul before the boulder was brought. She became an example for the believing men and women until the end of time. The angels shaded her with their wings.

The Pharaoh was an arrogant tyrant. Because she obeyed her Lord, Asiya was not affected by her husband's disbelief. Therefore, let it be known that God is the Just Judge, Who will not punish anyone except for his or her own sins.

It was reported that Asiya would ask, "Who prevailed?" When she was told Moses and Aaron, peace be upon them, prevailed. She said, "I believe in the Lord of Moses and Aaron."

MARY (MARYAM BINT IMRAN)

God chose Mary to be the purest woman in all the world. He dedicated an entire chapter of the Holy Qur'an to this noble woman.

Her mother's name was Hannah and her father was called Imran. This beautifully spiritual woman was born into a family of high lineage of great Prophets chosen by God, namely Adam, Noah, and Abraham, upon them be peace.

One day Hannah prayed, "My Lord, I have dedicated that which is in my womb to Your exclusive service. Accept it, then, from me. Surely You are the All-Hearing, the All-Knowing" (Al Imran 3:35).

When she gave birth to a female child, she named her Mary, may God be pleased with her. Hannah dedicated not only her daughter for the sake of God, but also prayed for her daughter's offspring to be protected from the curse of Satan.

Not only did God accept her offering, but He also made Mary grow in purity and beauty in the care of her guardian, Prophet Zachariah, peace be upon him. Whenever he entered her chambers, he found that she was supplied with food, drink, and fresh fruits that were out of season. Surprised, he asked her how such things came to her. Her reply was that they came from God; He provides sustenance to whom He pleases in abundance.

Since Zachariah and his wife had no children, and they had reached old age, seeing this miracle, he decided to pray to his Lord for a child: "My Lord, bestow upon me out of Your grace a good, upright offspring. Truly, You are the Hearer of

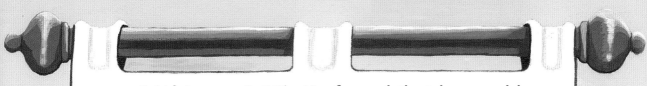

prayer" (Al Imran 3:38). He feared that he would pass away and that his community would forget about God. One day, as Zachariah was standing in prayer, an angel called to him: "God gives you the glad tidings of John, to confirm a Word from God, and as one lordly, perfectly chaste, a Prophet, among the righteous" (Al Imran 3:39). Zachariah asked for a sign from God. The sign that was given to him was that he was unable to speak to anyone for three days, and could only speak through sign language. Upon seeing this, the happy servant humbly glorified his Lord ever so deeply in prayer, morning and evening.

God sent the angel Gabriel in the form of a man to Mary. At first, he frightened her, and she said if you fear God, do not come near me. Gabriel reassured her: "I am only a messenger of your Lord to be a means (for God's gift) to you of a pure son" (Maryam 19:19).

"Mary, God has chosen you and made you pure, and exalted you above all the women in the world" (Al Imran 3:42). "Mary, God gives you the glad tidings of a Word from Him, to be called the Messiah, Jesus son of Mary; highly honored in the world and the Hereafter, and one of those near-stationed to God. He will speak to people in the cradle and in manhood, and he is of the righteous." "Lord," said Mary, "how shall I have a son seeing no mortal has ever touched me?" "That is how it is," he (Gabriel) said, "God creates whatever He wills;

when He decrees a thing, He does but say to it 'Be!' and it is" (Al Imran 3:45–47).

As Mary's pregnancy advanced, she went to a remote and secluded place. The pains of childbirth were so agonizing that they drove her to the trunk of a palm tree. In the middle of her labor she cried out, "Would that I had died before this, and had become a thing forgotten, completely forgotten!" (Maryam 19:23). She said this because she felt people would not understand where this baby boy came from. A voice cried to her from beneath the palm tree, "Do not grieve! Your Lord has set a rivulet at your feet. And shake the trunk of the date-palm towards you: it will drop fresh, ripe dates upon you." (Maryam 19:24–26). She was told not to speak to anyone, and soon, she brought the baby boy to her people. They said "O Mary! You have come for sure with an unheard of, mighty thing!" and reminded her of her noble family and the great honor they held: "... your father was never a wicked man, nor was your mother unchaste" (Maryam 19:27–28).

Mary said nothing, and simply pointed to her baby. They cried: "How can we talk to one in the cradle, an infant boy?" (Maryam 19:29). To their astonishment, the baby Jesus spoke. He said: "Surely I am *abdullah* (a servant of God). He (has already decreed that He) will give me the Book (the Gospel) and make me a Prophet. He has made me blessed (and a means of His blessings for people) wherever

I may be, and He has enjoined upon me the prayer (the *salah*) and the prescribed purifying alms (the *zakah*) (and to enjoin the same upon others) for as long as I live. And (He has made me) dutiful towards my mother, and He has not made me unruly, wicked. So peace be upon me on the day I was born and the day of my death, and the day when I will be raised to life" (Maryam 19:30–33).

During his Prophetic mission, Jesus performed many miracles. The Qur'an states that he said, "I have come to you with a clear proof from your Lord: I fashion for you out of clay something in the shape of a bird, then I breathe into it, and it becomes a bird by God's leave. And I heal the blind from birth and the leper, and I revive the dead, by God's leave" (Al Imran 3:49).

Neither Prophet Muhammad nor Prophet Jesus, peace and blessings be upon them, changed the basic principles of the belief in one God, which was a belief brought by earlier Prophets; they confirmed and renewed it. In the Holy Qur'an, Jesus is reported as saying that he came to attest the law that was before him, and to make lawful to mankind that which was forbidden. He said: "I have come to you with a clear proof (demonstrating that I am a Messenger of God) from your Lord. So keep from disobedience to God in due reverence for Him and piety, and obey me" (Al Imran 3:50).

God chose chaste, devout, and righteous Mary as the virgin mother of Jesus. Muslims respect and revere Prophet Jesus. They consider him one of the greatest of God's Messengers to mankind.

KHADIJA: DAUGHTER OF KHUWAYLID, WIFE OF THE PROPHET

Khadija bint Khuwaylid, may God be pleased with her, was the first person to embrace Islam. She was one who accepted without questioning or having doubt, one who dedicated herself and her wealth to Islam unconditionally.

She came from the family of the Quraysh, descendants of Prophet Ishmael, son of Prophet Abraham, which became a powerful merchant tribe controlling Mecca and the Ka'ba. She had been married twice before, and both of her husbands had died. She had two sons and a daughter from her previous marriages. She was extremely wealthy. Some say she was the wealthiest person of all the Quraysh. She managed her wealth wisely, hiring traders to take some of her money to buy goods abroad, sell them, and bring the wealth back. It was hard to find honest traders. When she heard of the trustworthiness of Muhammad, peace and blessings be upon him, she hired him to be one of her traders.

One day Khadija assigned her assistant, a man named Maysara, to travel with him. Maysara was amazed by his character and trustworthiness. When in Syria, he rested

under a tree, and a monk commented that none but a Prophet ever sat there.

The noble Prophet worked exceptionally hard. He took Khadija's money, bought goods, sold them, bought more goods, and sold them for more money. He came back with double the amount of profits Khadija was used to.

Maysara decided to do some matchmaking. He described all the virtues he possessed to Khadija. He then asked him, "Why don't you marry her?" His reply was that he did not have the means. Later, he gave his consent, and they were married. She was 40 years old, and he was 25. Khadija would give birth to six more children: Qasim, Zainab, Ruqayya, Umm Kulthum, Fatima, and Abdullah. Fatima is one of the four noble women in Islam.

After a few years, he started practicing seclusion. He went to the Cave of Hira in the city of Mecca, and stayed there in solitude and devotion, for as long as a whole month at times. Khadija supported him by sending him food, water, and someone to check up on him periodically.

When he was 40 and Khadija was 55, the first revelation came down to him from the angel Gabriel. He told him: "Read!" though he had never received any instruction in reading and writing. He said to the angel, "I am not a reader." The angel took hold of him, squeezed him as much as he could bear, and said again, "Read!" This continued several times.

"Read in the Name of your Lord, Who has created... Created human from a clot clinging (to the wall of the womb). Read, and your Lord is the All-Munificent, Who has taught (human) by the pen" (Alaq 96:1–4).

He ran home to Khadija from the Cave of Hira with a trembling heart. Looking pale, he said, "Wrap me up! Wrap me up!" She asked no questions, covered him with blankets, and comforted him. After a while, he told her what had happened.

She said: "Good tidings, O Muhammad! By Him in Whose hand is my soul, I believe that you are the Prophet of this community. God would never humiliate you, for you are good to your relatives, guests, and you answer the call of those who are in distress."

She took him to her old, blind, religious cousin, Waraqa ibn Nawfal, who had studied the Christian and Jewish scriptures thoroughly.

He asked him some questions, and then declared, "This is the same being who brought the revelations of God to Moses. God has chosen you, Muhammad, to be the Prophet of his people. They will call you a liar, they will persecute you, they will banish you, and they will fight against you. Oh, that I could live to see those days. I would fight with you." He then kissed his forehead.

After this incident, his destiny unfolded to him. In deep meditation and melancholy, he felt himself called by a voice from heaven to arise and preach the truth. "O, you cloaked one (who has preferred solitude)! Arise and warn! And declare your Lord's (indescribable and incomparable) greatness!" (Al-Muddathir 74:1–3).

He arose and engaged himself in the work to which he was called

(Prophethood). Khadija was the first to accept his mission, along with her entire household, including her two sons and daughter, Ali, Zayd, and Umm Ayman. They were to believe in the revelations of the Holy Qur'an, abandon the idolatry of their people, and offer prayers to God the Almighty.

Khadija told her husband, now a Prophet, to give up the trading business and dedicate himself entirely to the spreading of Islam. She donated her wealth for the sake of Islam, freeing slaves, helping the needy, and supporting the family. They were subjected to harsh living conditions, because there was a social and economic boycott against them and all of the believers. They were exiled and forced to a ravine outside Mecca. They could have lived alone with just her wealth and house, but she stayed and supported God's Messenger by living with him. She was a patient woman with two sons who died in infancy. She was near starvation and sometimes ate grass. Abu Huraira reported that on one occasion the angel Gabriel came to the Prophet and said, "O Messenger of God! Khadija is coming with a bowl of soup for you. When she comes to you, give her greetings of peace from her Lord and from me, and give her the good news of a palace of jewels in Paradise, where there will neither be any noise nor any tiredness."

Khadija, the mother of the believers, died when she was 65 years old. The Prophet was so sad at her death, and the death of his supportive uncle Abu Talib, who died in the same year, that he called it "the Year of Grief."

After twenty-five years of marriage, the Prophet did not marry again for three years, even at the encouragement of others. He delivered food to her friends every time he slaughtered a lamb. She had a special place in our beloved Prophet's heart.

FATIMA: DAUGHTER OF THE PROPHET AND KHADIJA

Fatima bint Muhammad, may God be pleased with her, was the fifth child of our Prophet and Khadija. She was born at a time when her noble father had begun to spend long periods of time in the solitude of the mountains around Mecca, meditating and reflecting on the mysteries of creation. Fatima became lonely as she saw her older sisters leave home one after another to live with their husbands. When she was five, she heard that her father became *Rasulullah* (the Messenger of God). His first task was to convey the good news of Islam to his family and close relations. "Worship God alone" was the message. Her mother, who was a tower of strength and support, explained to Fatima what her father had to do. From that time on, she became more closely attached to him, and felt a deep and abiding love for him.

Often she was at his side, walking through the narrow streets and alleys of Mecca. They visited the Ka'ba or attended secret gatherings of the early Muslims who had accepted Islam and pledged allegiance to the Prophet.

Polytheism (idol worship and thus associating partners with God) was deeply rooted in the Quraysh people. They had personal interests in the pagan old ways of worship. Their prestige was dependent upon its maintenance. They foolishly asked: "Which of you can bring the entrails of a slaughtered animal, and throw it on Muhammad?"

God's Messenger and his Companions were forced to flee to an arid valley with limited supplies of food. Fatima was

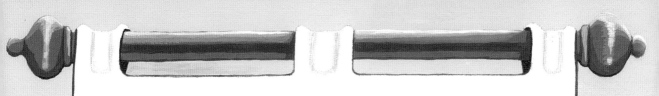

twelve years old, one of the youngest members of the group. She had to undergo months of hardship and suffering. This was the year in which the noble Khadija, and later Abu Talib, died: "The Year of Grief." Fatima was a young lady, greatly distressed by her mother's death. She wept bitterly, and for some time, was so grief-stricken that her health deteriorated. It was even feared she might die herself.

Often the trials were too much for her. Once, around this time, an insolent mob heaped dust and earth upon the Prophet's gracious head. As he entered his home, Fatima wept profusely as she wiped the dust from her father's head. "Do not cry, my daughter," he said, "for God shall protect your father."

Fatima, may God be pleased with her, was given the title of *Az-Zahra*, which means "The Resplendent One." This was because of her beaming face, which seemed to radiate light. Much of her time was spent in *salah* (prayer), reading the Qur'an, and other acts of worship. Fatima had a strong resemblance to her father. Aisha, a later wife of the Prophet, said of her: "I have not seen any one of God's creatures resemble the Messenger of God in speech, conversation, and manner of sitting more than Fatima bint Muhammad."

When the Prophet saw her approaching, he welcomed her by standing up, kissing her, taking her by the hand, and sitting down with her in the place where he was sitting. She did the same upon the Prophet approaching her.

Fatima's fine manners and gentle speech were part of her lovely and endearing personality. She was especially kind to poor and indigent people, and gave all the food she had to those in need while she herself remained hungry. She inherited from her father a persuasive eloquence rooted in wisdom. When she spoke, people were moved to tears. Their hearts were filled with gratitude to God for His grace and endless bounties.

One day, Ali, the son of Abu Talib and the nephew of our beloved Prophet, built up enough courage to ask the Prophet for Fatima's hand in marriage. He was very shy, and finally the Prophet suggested, "Perhaps you have come to propose marriage to Fatima." Many Companions of the Prophet had proposed. However, the Prophet said, "I await the order of my Lord," for Fatima and Ali had a special place in his heart. When the Prophet asked, "What money do you have?" Ali replied, "I have my sword, shield, and the clothes I wear." The Prophet said, "You cannot do without your sword, with which you defend Islam and remove hardship from the Messenger of God, but give me your shield." The shield was sold for 500 dirham, which was the marriage dowry (*mahr*) of Fatima, who accepted Ali as her husband. Ali was also one of the first people to embrace Islam.

Fatima was about nineteen years old and Ali was twenty-one. The Prophet performed the marriage ceremony himself. At the *walimah* (marriage banquet), the guests were served dates, figs, and *hais*, a mixture of dates and butter fat. A leading member of the *Ansar* (helpers of the Muslims) donated a ram for the wedding, and others made offerings of grain. Historians have said that the Prophet did not want Fatima to leave

him even after her marriage, and so she lived in the house next to his, which he could enter from his own.

To the great joy of all the believers, Fatima gave birth to a boy in the month of Ramadan the third year after the *Hijra* (migration from Mecca to Medina). The Prophet spoke the words of the *adhan* (call to prayer) into the newborn baby's ear, and then called him Hasan, the beautiful one. One year later, she gave birth to another son who was called Husayn, which means "little Hasan (the little beautiful one)." Fatima often brought her two sons to see their grandfather, who was very fond of them. They climbed on his back when he prostrated in prayer.

At the Battle of the Ditch, a battle against the disbelievers, Fatima led the Muslim women in prayer; on that place there stands Masjid Fatima, one of seven mosques where the Muslims stood guard.

One year, the angel Gabriel recited the Qur'an to the Prophet twice. This was unusual and caused the Prophet to realize his time was coming to an end. So he summoned Fatima, kissed her, and whispered into her ear. She wept. Then he whispered again in her ear and she smiled. Upon the question, "What did the Messenger of God say to you?" Fatima said: "He first told me that he would meet his Lord after a short while, so I cried. Then he said, 'Don't cry, for you will be the first of my household to join me.' So I laughed."

The Prophet had a special love for Fatima. He once said, "Fatima is a part of me. Whoever upsets her, upsets me."